Pebble Plus

Exploremos la galaxia/Exploring the Galaxy

Mercurio/Mercury

por/by Thomas K. Adamson

Traducción/Translation: Martín Luis Guzmán Ferrer, Ph.D.
Editor Consultor/Consulting Editor: Dra. Gail Saunders-Smith

James Gerard, Consultant
Aerospace Education Specialist, NASA
Kennedy Space Center, Florida

Capstone press

Mankato, Minnesota

Pebble Plus is published by Capstone Press
151 Good Counsel Drive, P.O. Box 669, Mankato, Minnesota 56002
http://www.capstone-press.com

1 2 3 4 5 6 11 10 09 08 07 06

Library of Congress Cataloging-in-Publication Data
Adamson, Thomas K.
    [Mercury. Spanish & English]
    Mercurio = Mercury / by Thomas K. Adamson.
    p. cm.—(Pebble plus: Exploremos la galaxia = Exploring the galaxy)
    English and Spanish.
    Includes index.
    ISBN-13: 978-0-7368-5881-6 (hardcover)
    ISBN-10: 0-7368-5881-4 (hardcover)
    1. Mercury (Planet)—Juvenile literature. I. Title: Mercury. II. Title. III. Series.
QB611.A3318 2005
523.41—dc22   2005019033

Summary: Simple text and photographs describe the planet Mercury.

Editorial Credits
Mari C. Schuh, editor; Kia Adams, designer; Alta Schaffer, photo researcher; Eida del Risco, Spanish copy editor; Jenny Marks, bilingual editor

Photo Credits
Digital Vision, 5 (Venus)
NASA, 4 (Pluto), 13, 15; JPL, 5 (Jupiter); JPL/Caltech, 5 (Uranus), 11, 17
PhotoDisc Inc., cover, 4 (Neptune), 5 (Mars, Mercury, Earth, Sun, Saturn); 9 (both), 19; Stock Trek, 1; PhotoDisc Imaging, 7
Photo Researchers/Frank Zullo, 21

Note to Parents and Teachers

The Exploremos la galaxia/Exploring the Galaxy series supports national standards related to earth and space science. This book describes Mercury in both English and Spanish. The photographs support early readers and language learners in understanding the text. Repetition of words and phrases helps early readers and language learners learn new words. This book also introduces early readers to subject-specific vocabulary words, which are defined in the Glossary section. Early readers may need assistance to read some words and to use the Table of Contents, Glossary, Internet Sites, and Index sections of the book.

Table of Contents

Mercury 4

Mercury's Size 8

Mercury's Surface 10

People and Mercury 18

Glossary 22

Internet Sites 24

Index 24

Tabla de contenidos

Mercurio 4

El tamaño de Mercurio 8

La superficie de Mercurio 10

La gente y La Tierra 18

Glosario 23

Sitios de Internet 24

Índice 24

Mercury

Mercury is the closest planet to the Sun. Mercury moves around the Sun faster than any other planet.

Mercurio

Mercurio es el planeta más cercano al Sol. Mercurio se mueve alrededor del Sol más rápido que cualquiera de los otros planetas.

The Solar System/El sistema solar

Mercury/Mercurio

Sun/El Sol

Mercury can be colder than
a freezer at night. Mercury
can be hotter than an oven
during the day.

Por la noche Mercurio puede
ser tan frío como un congelador.
Por el día Mercurio puede ser tan
caliente como un horno.

Mercury's Size

Mercury is the second smallest
planet. Earth is three times
wider than Mercury.

El tamaño de Mercurio

Mercurio es el segundo
planeta más pequeño.
La Tierra es tres veces
más ancha que Mercurio.

Earth/La Tierra

Mercury/Mercurio

Mercury's Surface

Mercury is a rocky planet.
The surface of Mercury
looks like Earth's moon.

La superficie de Mercurio

Mercurio es un planeta
rocoso. La superficie
de Mercurio se parece
a la luna de la Tierra.

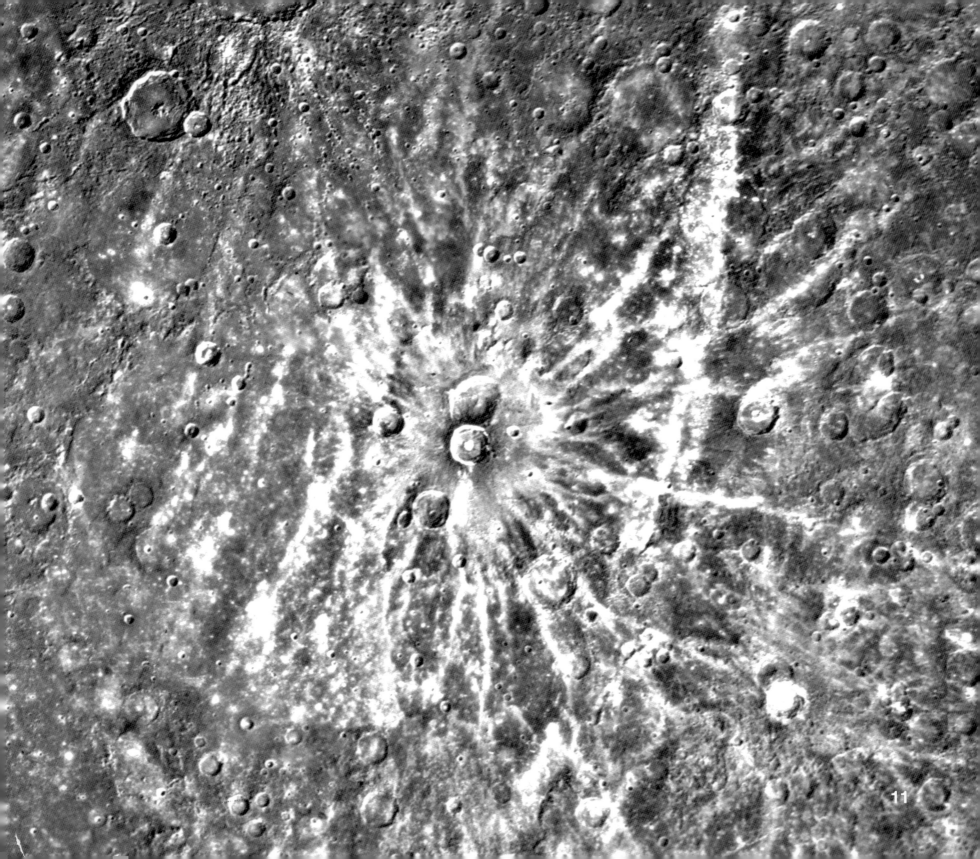

Mercury's surface looks gray.
Dust covers the surface.

La superficie de Mercurio
parece gris. La superficie
está cubierta de polvo.

Craters cover Mercury's surface. Large rocks called asteroids made these holes.

La superficie de Mercurio está cubierta de cráteres. Unas enormes rocas llamadas asteroides hicieron estos hoyos.

Craters near the planet's
poles have ice. Sunlight
cannot shine on the ice
to melt it.

Los cráteres cercanos a los
polos del planeta tienen hielo.
La luz solar no puede brillar
sobre el hielo para derretirlo.

17

People and Mercury

Mercury does not have
air or water. People
and animals could not
live on Mercury.

La gente y Mercurio

Mercurio no tiene
agua ni aire. La gente
y los animales no podrían
vivir en Mercurio.

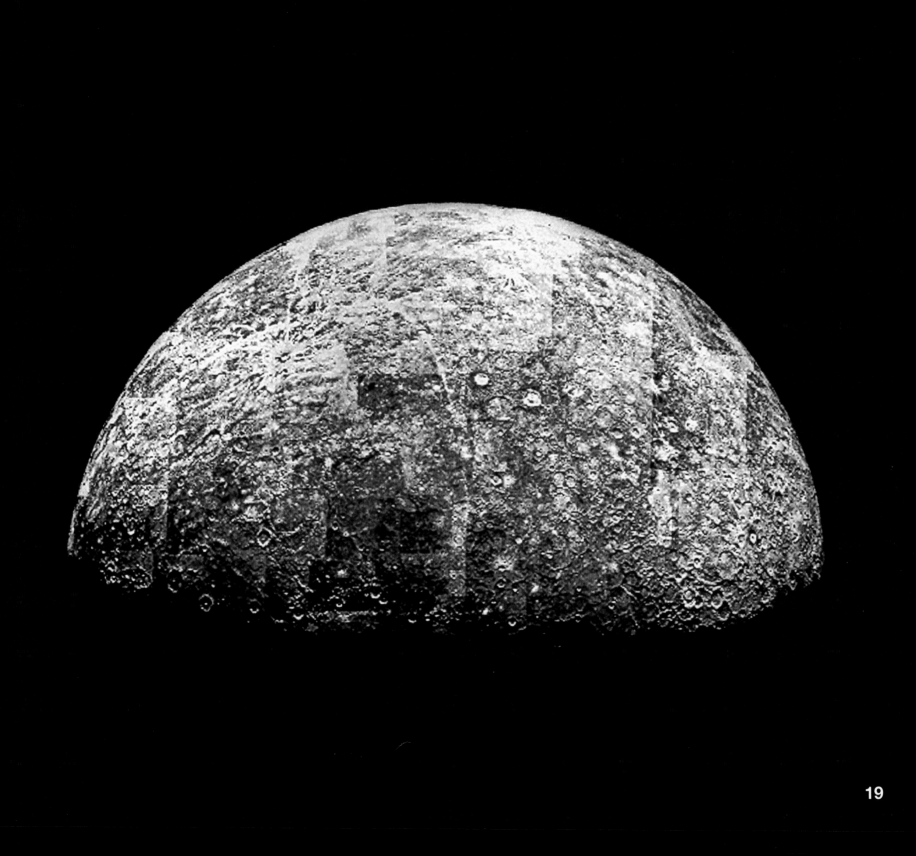

People can sometimes
see Mercury from Earth.
Mercury looks like a dim star.

La gente algunas veces puede
ver a Mercurio desde la Tierra.
Mercurio parece una estrella opaca.

Mercury/
Mercurio →

Glossary

asteroid—a large space rock that moves around the Sun

crater—a large bowl-shaped hole in the ground

dim—somewhat dark; dim stars are not very bright.

moon—an object that moves around a planet; Earth has one moon; Mercury does not have any moons.

planet—a large object that moves around the Sun; Mercury is the closest planet to the Sun.

pole—the top or bottom part of a planet

star—a large ball of burning gases in space; the Sun is a star.

Sun—the star that the planets move around; the Sun provides light and heat for the planets.

Glosario

asteroide—un gran pedazo de roca espacial que se mueve alrededor del Sol

cráter—un hoyo en la tierra en forma de bol

estrella—una enorme bola de gases ardientes en el espacio; el Sol es una estrella.

luna—un objeto que se mueve alrededor de un planeta; la Tierra tiene una luna; Mercurio no tiene ninguna luna.

opaca—un tanto oscura; las estrellas opacas no son muy brillantes.

planeta—un objeto grande que se mueve alrededor del Sol; la Tierra es el tercer planeta a partir del Sol; Mercurio es el planeta más cercano al Sol.

polo—la parte de arriba o de abajo de un planeta

Sol—la estrella alrededor de la cual se mueven los planetas; el Sol les proporciona luz y calor a los planetas.

Internet Sites

Do you want to find out more about Mercury and the solar system? Let FactHound, our fact-finding hound dog, do the research for you.

Here's how:

1) Visit **www.facthound.com**

2) Type in the **Book ID** number: **0736821147**

3) Click on **FETCH IT**.

FactHound will fetch Internet sites picked by our editors just for you!

Sitios de Internet

¿Quieres saber más sobre Mercurio y el sistema solar? Deja que FactHound, nuestro perro sabueso, haga la investigación por ti.

Así:

1) Ve a **www.facthound.com**

2) Teclea el número ID del libro: **0736821147**

3) Clic en **FETCH IT**.

¡Facthound buscará en los sitios de Internet que han seleccionado nuestros editores sólo para ti!

Index

air, 18

asteroids, 14

craters, 14, 16

dust, 12

Earth, 8, 10, 20

holes, 14

ice, 16

moon, 10

night, 6

planet, 4, 8, 10, 16

rocks, 14

star, 20

Sun, 4

sunlight, 16

surface, 10, 12, 14

water, 18

Índice

agua, 18

aire, 18

asteroides, 14

cráteres, 14, 16

estrella, 20

hielo, 16

hoyos, 14

luna, 10

luz solar, 16

noche, 6

planeta, 4, 8, 10, 16

polvo, 12

rocas, 14

Sol, 4

superficie, 10, 12, 14

Tierra, 8, 10, 20